This edition published in 2012 by
House of Anansi Press Inc.
110 Spadina Avenue, Suite 801
Toronto, ON, M5V 2K4
Tel. 416-363-4343
Fax 416-363-1017
www.anansi.ca

Distributed in Canada by
HarperCollins Canada Ltd.
1995 Markham Road
Scarborough, ON, M1B 5M8
Toll free tel. 1-800-387-0117

Distributed in the United States by
Publishers Group West
1700 Fourth Street
Berkeley, CA 94710
Toll free tel. 1-800-788-3123

House of Anansi Press is committed to protecting our natural environment. As part of our efforts, the interior of this book is printed on paper that contains 100% post-consumer recycled fibres, is acid-free, and is processed chlorine-free.

16 15 14 13 12   1 2 3 4 5

LIBRARY AND ARCHIVES CANADA CATALOGING IN PUBLICATION
Moure, Erín, 1955–
The unmemntioable / Erín Moure.

Poems.
ISBN 978-1-77089-004-6
I. Title.

PS8576.O96U56 2012   C811'.54   C2011-904017-4

Library of Congress Control Number: 2011929949

Cover design: Erín Moure
Text design: Erín Moure
Typesetting: Laura Brady

We acknowledge for their financial support of our publishing program the Canada Council for the Arts, the Ontario Arts Council, and the Government of Canada through the Canada Book Fund.

Printed and bound in Canada

Procedure 1) Poet (anyone) sits behind curtain or gate and recites page of text individually to listeners, who sit without seeing. 2) Listeners return one by one until entire text is read. 3) Each then shares with the others what was heard. a) The native people rose up and killed the interlopers. b) The nation drove the interlopers out. c) All on the verges endured the sorrows. 4) Silence. 5) She stood in the rain and birches holding a spoon of ashes. Experience (Adorno) (blinded) *E. Sampedrín*
****

Cover image: Singing Jars, a detail from *Preserves* (2010), an installation/performance by Vida Simon in the At Home Gallery, Šamorín, Slovakia. Photo by Vida Simon.

Ce visage qui devait être la seule image du temps de paix à traverser le temps
de guerre, il se demanda longtemps s'il l'avait vraiment vu,
ou s'il avait crée ce moment de douceur
pour étayer le moment de folie qui allait venir.

Chris Marker, *La Jetée*

rattle

We challenged the dice, became travellers of mirages. (Oana Avasilichioaei)

The land of your mother wanders
everywhere, like language.

*Das land deiner Mutter, es wandert
überallhin, wie die Sprache.*

Paul Celan, *1963*

Like the cataclysm's first name.
Like chagrin's first companion, error.
Dreamed all night of _____.

Held out the crevasse of my hands for water

Home: the barbaric language.
I wade through the stream of grasses.
My mother's sweater clings to their seeds
I bow down to soil and streaming grasses
Light's hedge and memory

I see her wading in those grasses
outside memory, inside soil
her frail membrane
touches, what it touches <hillside> <touches>
disappears

(E.M., daughter of M. Grędysz,
daughter of А. Хамуляк)

To *enfant* book and word. The word that can be lost and burned. The word that cannot <shibboleth>. The very birth of language.

A row of houses leads to the Davydivka River. "Those were Polish houses." No, not *these*, *these* are new.

They burned those Polish houses, and drove them away.

Who this them was. This they. They/this/them.
(rain)
(silence of rain)
(we walk behind the woman who is not speaking)

Now they wish they would come back again.
(a pronoun problem)
(a time problem)
(a village silence)
<infans>

Down to the river behind the school we walked

our books strapped together droppt in wet grass above
[i wanted to marry you]

a forbidden surface <unmemntioable>

[a vowel in ttrout]

In the fields where people were once murdered on the basis of an accent. By asking locals the names for food, *pyrohy* or *pirogy*, they knew which language led at home, which is to say, at the table.

To say the name of food one way =
"the historical enemies of the x <scratch> people."

Yet there was another name for the people of this place.
тутешні. *Tuteshni*. *Tutejszy*. "The ones who live here." Local.

Torch the homes (they won't come back *here*, but vanish as *I* does)
Torch the homes (cut out the tongue, excise the barbaric accent)

(South Africa)
(Galicia)
(Dominican Republic) (southeast of L'viv)

panic. pandemonium. pâine. (broyt). chleb. хліб. bread.

(don't leave a single fruit tree ~~standing~~)

At night the children were harvested with flames.
The building spontaneously combusted.

How did it burn down? we ask the woman, standing
at the empty grove, rain pasting our clothes flat.
It was made of wood, she says.

She calls it not x but y, the word from the other tongue that is this
tongue too, a village tongue, a word from the
expelled language _____

The infiltrations are lexical: silence, blood, aire.

[spear trout with sticks of white grass, larvae]

Marked by that foreign word, marked too by imperial consequence
and time, peeled from the mud of labour, s_rr_w too
harvested of v_wels
f_r tr_ut

, dad <táto> came in and whispered to me to say (for ever after)—
ukrainian <mom> матінка, мама, мати

Máhtinka, máma, máty

"They came down the road at night and pitted us against our
brothers."

So as not to be killed.

[trout lay in the shadow of trees breathing in shallow water]

There are places on the skin where passivity lies as tremendous as light.

I woke up among the fallen petals.

Nostalgia. The word no one will admit to.

The best protection against fire, some say, is that old growth has already burnt.

That and—today—"social being." It is the necromancy of denying fear.

Walking at night out of the forest....

"no such design offered itself up" (C.D. Wright)

(scythe)

After supper the families are back in the fields with hand implements and bicycles, making use of the light.

thereI left dust your dust
as soil, and you left soil in me
and soilI took in equal measure
soil that fed me, and my heart
was shoulder and картопля and
капуста (a leaf for my head)
and breviary mostlyI was soldier of your soldier
eye of your eye
and your blindness my blind
shoulder my shoulder
shape was your shape
and so we shaped
so that shape could induce us
in rain, in wet ends of buildings
in sand and soil whereI
scooped soil mother daughter

and stepped out of "Polish" trees, I famished.

soft pears fall from these trees
soft fruit in the mouth and cheekbone
soft bones of the mouth
soft fruit and light no one will remember

Relationships written down instead of remembered, cuts the tie.
When the register burns so does memory as this was passed to
writing and the content of a writing burned can no longer be
handed back to memory, for writing abolishes memory and as what
was written can no longer be passed down, it has no Author in the old
sense: no ability *to act as proxy to, to verify on behalf of.*

Анастасія and Tomasz, authors, vanish.

In grasses and herbs waist high, wick-wet to the waist, digging the
small hole for the ashes of my mother, in this act in Великі Глібовичі
I enfant myself, I enact as I was enacted, *infans*, I assume the
question in the grass for as many and as few years as are left to me.

Is that you, E.S., staring at me in the trees?

(the scythes)

(the scythes) Perhaps it is better if Elisa Sampedrín writes of these things. She Galician not of Halychyna or the Krai or Kresy, not of the verges but of Brigantium Flavium, rúa dos Xudeos, who gets off the train from Bucureşti at Великі Глібовичі to find Erín Moure burying the ashes of her mother, in the grove where once a latin church stood. E.S. bows her head of course; ashes are going to the ground again. Opening the earth is not always a crime. That a mother was born in Poland because of the magnates and a League of Nations, with a Polish name or perhaps Ukrainian, yet speaking the languages of the *village*. "Local" for centuries. "From here." Tuteszny. Тутешні.

In those years, a name was an enemy, an accent in a word was an enemy, an alphabetic spire of ink in a ledger was an enemy.

I come from nowhere, she'd say to the small E.M.
Some people come from nowhere.

Remedia Amoris

Her eyes'
indigence a ballad frenzy to the core

look back optic
human will

to see and objects rise from
their own properties

nowhere
memoria amoris et gloriae voluptas

E.S.
București

Yet we know that what the tip of the white cane touches is processed in the visual area of the brain. Touch and sight merge. The brain doesn't care what body or prosthesis act as conduit for sight. The skin too.

[Take me in your arms] a way of seeing then. [There is nothing natural.] A sense organ

"E., Forgive Me"

The book is the history of comets, as
seen by children.

The book is the history of the sun and moon in
1944: "Soarele este ochiul lui Dumnezeu."

1963: Don't drink water during an eclipse.

2010: The sun can't wear the world's
shoes.

E.S.
București

1 / 2

This is the first time I have ever written in the dark. Wherever there will be nothing, *dearest trout*, read that I love you.

Voilà la première fois que j'écris dans les ténèbres. Partout où il n'y aura rien, lisez que je vous aime.

Denis Diderot, *1759*

If anything, it's the fault of reading. When Chus Pato's poetry appeared on my desk, I decided to give up writing poems. I moved to Bucureşti to see if I could free myself from this crisis of experience, this excision of language. Then I saw Erín Moure in the park at a café table, looking at me. Why did she come here?

What does she know about experience? Her mother tongues resist all attempts at a technical language.

Is it that she has no mother tongue?

Today, I refuse to be pinned down to an identity. Right away, I want to betray it.

Infamy's gesture: author of this.

E.S. looks out at the church on Str. Matei Voievod, Bucureşti. The lights of an ambulance flash off the darkness of the walls. Siren. She sets down the pen and puts her fingers into her hair to hold her head still. Why did I write this, she thinks

(the scythes)

I came to this Eastern capital with my preconceptions and had no idea what it is to live here. I wanted to be awed or horrified by boulevards, wanted *gris* in my eyes; I mangled Ceauşescu on the tongue, entered theatres at dusk and emerged in night's pulse, lips charred with the calyxes of girls and coffee. I am drawn to this hive of the East because its clamours roil me. In my notebooks, streets die, mongrels give birth, virginity is fouled again and again, birds come out on bright tiled roofs and sing. I came to not be in Ukraine. My room looks across at one of those roofs, and in the morning I hear its birds. "There are persons who can speak no more"

(cauterized)

I came with my preconceptions. I thought I would excise poetry, cast down the dice unread.

E. should have stayed in Ukraine or Canada.
She has no business wanting to know me.

Medicamina Faciei Femineae

Body (the illegible dis-guesture) enfronts all
language. a Body not
even accounted for—or constrained—by
this word "body" which wills or bodes its own remnant to
> detach—from neural bliss—
> a thick layer of cells
> *que se despregan*, creating, thus,
> context. (which is the body

> come loose, dislodged,

inadherable, malsain, rotted, dross, snot, lichen,
tomb, drift, ambivalent, auganeve, pus, fog, urine, šaltibarščai,
snow

E.S.
Bucureşti

Fasti

I wanted to stop crying out like this
before emigration
I wanted to shout ice cream
Climbed up a narrow crevice hastened
by light
a true bit of the story came on a bird
a true bit of the story came on a tiny clove
carved with a pin
I pushed it into the hole in my jaw
<the sky>

so it has touched we, that neuralgic point of extinction <wreck>

we will not hear ten voices
we will scrap history
what ordinary translator <translate> outlasts human fear?
completely incinerate my _____
does not endure
does not extinguish
ill be gain or forfeit, stricken
pales, stokes aversion
to regret

ice cream! ice cream!

E.S.
București

22

A subject speaks (amid the trees). Is that experience?

Or is speech a subject's very constitution and assembly, which then makes experience possible. "Subjectivity is nothing more than the aptitude of the speaker to posit its self as *ego*: it is in no way definable by a feeling an individual might hold in their 'inner forum' or 'sanctum'."

Having no inner forum suits me just fine. In me there is no inner law. Agamben's "in no way" lies quietly in my mouth beside "definable," pushing it sideways. ~~When I kissed her~~

the cord of the voice entered my body from her mouth, passing over the back of the tongue, its ligament, and down the esophagus or bronchi, piercing to the genitals.

(laughting
(laughter
(gen-esis
~~trout~~]

Je n'ai pas de vie intérieure, c'est le monde qui m'intéresse.

Somnium

It still proceeds from the same *I think*

In search of the transcendental operations of the experience of
I think
a core drowned in the *I think*
experience already refers to the *I think*
The synthesis accomplished by the unity of the *I think*, behind
experience

Experience which in the final analysis is not the "I think"
Nevertheless, the *I think*
any ideal tie and any synthesis, *I think*

this is not a pure derision
nor a simple failure of experience
it is the modality of the unmemntioable taking on meaning
the Cartesian paradox of the idea of the infinite, blinded in me

Doors screen wet canvas not admit smoke scanted air to face

I have returned for child and I was told to leave on cart

Told to stomach bayonet or disavow my brother carted off as Pole

He liked horses, knew to plough. He was known to celebrate <get on> with horses <apt>

Also Ukrainians were incinerated who hid or married we

Poison seed of <grain of> hate in <to> its <her> family house of two

This good person has accompanied me to arbour light of tree

If counted surely anybody would return, I wait on horses trumpet shelter night

Field breaks child of crust to shirt blood <dry> blind

No one returned

Heroides

After the snows, we dug a hole in the roots where we could hide, for any trace of our own feet would betray us. We sat in the hole all winter; when we emerged on the track near Hucisko, people ran from us. We were no longer alive, no longer human. Oracles of the ambulant, we were visible (the air went coarse around us) but we could not be seen.

If experience is authority, is it not also blindness? Do objects rise?

E.S.
Bucureşti
in search of th

The Photographer of emigrants.
The Little Tailor.
The Glazier.
The Shroud Maker.
The Carpenter.
Son of David and Leah.
Died of hunger in '43.
The Baker.
The Rope Maker.
The Shirt Maker.
Died of hunger in Szwirsz in '42.
Refugee from Poland.
The Shoe Maker.
Brewer.
Burned alive in the forest.
Candle Maker.
Brick Maker.
Scribe. Harrier. Maker of Ataras.
Daughter of Izak. The Miller.
The Printer. The Water Carrier.
Died in the snow from eating bark off trees without first boiling.
Died at the sandpit, betrayed by the one who brought them food.

Near Huallen AB (night whispers Nelly Tom) those years of war
(scribe) (scribben) love blots out its name
          (fears Марія Анна Jozef Aleks Leon Jan) lost or gone
Where no one remains to make what is to be sold in towns
          (Billy Ken Erín how can any of us grow ~~old~~)

The texture of the paper infects the nib. "The fields moved like this for days." If I were you, I would turn the page now. There is no more to be gleaned here. What is it that you want to know? וואָס איז עס וואָס איר ווילט וויסן?

What is that Erín Moure writing at her café table? In a Moleskine Volant, black cover. Bought in Humanitas, Calea Victoriei, I bet. Bucharest is a city of contradictions, she is thinking. As someone does, not recognizing that she herself is contradictory. Streets are dug up. Under the streets, they found another city, a parallel city. All this time, the București under the ground thought of itself as București, and it was the 16th century.

Traders of hides. Brewers. Carts and smoke.

Who entered? Who drank early? Who combed silence out of their hair? Mother! Mother of Kant, antidote to romanticism!

(awaiting the invention of the streetcar
(awaiting the invention of the gas light
(awaiting the dog days of August

(awaiting the invention of the air conditioner

In her spires of ink: "The impossibility of leaving the other alone with the mystery of death. This way of laying claim to me, of calling me into question, this responsibility for the death of my (m)other, is a significance so irreducible that it is from it that the meaning of death may be understood.

Responsibility here is no dictate but all the gravity of love of the neighbour upon which the congenital meaning of that word love rests and which every literary form of its sublimation or profanation (I, je, eu) presupposes.
E. Lévinas, 'Notes on Meaning' (maybe)

The grave is not a refuge. Dearest trout. The debt remains."

Amores

I do not think that
Nevertheless, I think that
I have tried to pass
I have always attempted to look
I was taken one day
I found myself surrounded

It is from this idea that I have even understood
I have never sufficiently developed
I have tried to define it otherwise
I substitute for comprehension

I might be entirely I
More I than I myself
If in a certain moment, the I arises
I am not interested
I still remain I
I do not know if you may speak of hope

In the infinity of this *you* the I arises, against which death can do nothing:

E.S.
București

1 / 3

Only the idea of the infinite, *dearest trout,*
makes realism possible.

Seule l'idée de l'infini rend possible
le réalisme.

Emmanuel Lévinas, *1986*

When I first saw Elisa Sampedrín on the terrasse of Cafepedia (38°c) on Str. Verona, she was reading *Călătorii imaginare*, by E.A. Poe, in the Cotrău translation. The page open to a Chus Pato favourite: "Povestea lui Arthur Gordon Pym". Later, on the terrasse of the Persian restaurant (38.6°c), Str. Avalenşei 21, colţ cu Timpuri Noi, I saw E.S. again.

"Where is Elisa Sampedrín? Certainly not in the laconic notes that register her presence in the archive of infamy. Nor is she outside the archive, in a biographical reality which we can claim to know. She stands on the threshold of the text in which she is put into play, or, rather, her absence, her infinite turning away, is marked on the outer edge, a gesture that both renders her possible and exceeds and nullifies her intention."

Giorgio Agamben, Profanations, *altered and a few pages later, bracketed:*

"The author's gesture (E.M.) guarantees the life of the work (40.1°c) only through the irreducible presence of an inexpressive Outer Edge (E.S.)."

(39.4°c, 11 p.m., Str. Negustari)

The next day I saw Sampedrín in a church, cooling her heels in the shade under an icon of the Virgin holding a Christ who is a tiny man with the haircut of a stockbroker. Her fez cocked sideways and she was smoking a roll of paper. Startled I went out into the blaring sun quickly vanishing one side of my face then my arm and chest and leg into the white hot glare of Bucharest.

I left her a note.
Elisa: Green Horses on the Wall, Str. Matei Voievod, nr. 90, 7 p.m.

She didn't show up. I drank one коньяк. As if I were still in Ukraine.
She still didn't show up. I drank another коньяк, to tell the truth. When
I settled the bill, the barman gave me a note with my change, looking at
me oddly:

"Mais cette rupture n'interrompt pas l'identité de la personne. Alors que
l'accord entre Moi et Autrui—entre camarades, entre amis, entre
amants—ne peut supprimer la séparation. La résistance de l'Autre au
Même, c'est l'échec de la philosophie." (*Liberté et commandement*, E.
Lévinas)

I tucked the change into my wallet and the torn spires of ink into my
notebook. The barman had stopped scrutinizing me. He'd already
forgotten I'd ever been there.

I rattled the dice in Bucharest. When I cast them down, the word was already written. In an absolutely still blue sky

—RECULEGERE—

Corn and basil laid on the face of the god, to give thanks for the visible. The Museum, storehouse of the visible. I creep alongside curved and hewn wood, an entire church of wood in a huge hall of the autochthonous palace. In front or over the sides (for the roof is open), I look in. An incongruity: near the back of the church on the wall or vertical field, a white rough shirt hangs on a hanger, arms fallen.

(nearby, on a tiny plaque, translated slowly)

"We have enriched the church with a shirt."

Incongruity-enrichment. Anachronism, "un síntoma en el saber." Corn and basil.

"I wanted you to be born" <a voice>

"thanks, mom" <   >

Cafepedia and stinging heat (39°c). She is pretty mad at me. She doesn't want to talk to me, particularly. Something in her insists on separation—she has excised poetry and is researching "experience," and has decided Bucharest is the locale where experience is closest to the surface. Without experience, is there an "I"? How to speak of the experience of the "eu," the "je," the "я," the "I"? Can we speak of them at once? If, in translation, there is a difficulty with "je," isn't there even more so with "I"? Je pense, donc je suis. Is this also the unmemntioable? A breach or symptom? A kiss? The chord that enters the body?

I should have stayed in Ukraine, in the wound or crevice where I found myself, in the grove at Великі Глібовичі, a spoon of ashes, river.

After all, why feign optimism? Why ignite the core of human singularity? The old growth is burnt, they say. Why speak of it here?

Did E. really follow me to my mother's village? To the soldiers' road through Great Hlibovychi, its memory of burned houses? Of locked trains with chalked names of towns, heading north through the length of it, the ones who tore out, the ones who cried silently by?

Corn and basil on the face of stone.

Through my Bucharest hotel window wafts the acrid sweet burn of sugar. There's vanity in the trees. I remember my first long day on the train from Ukraine, hours drinking горілка with the folk dancers from Rivne (Erín! Drink!.... Sergei! No drink!) and I'm tired. That new restaurant DaDa on Strada M.V., nr. 94, I keep thinking I'll see E.S. there. I'll stroll past the terrasse, maybe she'll walk in for sarmale cu mămăligă under the green and white awning, amid copious flowers. Micul Paris, they once called Bucharest. Little Paris. Later E.S. laughs and sips a wine the colour of late afternoon light on the stones of L'viv, wears a dress I saw in a window in Zurich last August.

There's no vanity in the trees. I don't see E.S. It's not true I thought of her in Zurich. Window shut, I slept off the memory of the dancers' vodka. I was never in Zurich. She sent no message. My train was southbound. My mouth bled. She never came.

The philosopher Lévinas insists that the idea of the infinite in us consists in a paradox: thinking more than what has yet been thought.

The infinite is not my-idea-of-the-infinite because it exceeds every object of thought, including its own idea in me.

Thus thought cannot be constrained in "je" or "I" alone.

Thus ex-plosivity across membranes. A touch. E.S. and her prosthetic gesture: language. For if thought that exceeds what has yet been thought were not possible, the infinite would not be possible, and self/ itself or subjectivity its intermediary transcendence/ incendiaryy

wooudl collpase.

What is the infinite? In Great Hlibovychi, there is but clodded clay and ashes, sodden with rain. Freed now from the coercion of armies. From human trains and conflagrations. And on the hills now empty, from the cavernous broken barns of collectivization.

What is an entry into language? In it, we say "desire for love." But where to go from there? Most of this desire is unmemntioable. "Her dress" is provocative of enormous wells of sadness. The way through? Tears?

As D. says, "Perhaps the eye is destined not to see but to weep."

In the cemetery in Великі Глібовичі I stood surrounded by trees and grasses in the rain. An access to the infinite? An origin? The place where interior and exterior collpse?

Decades later, other fields (close by) dug delicately divulged their bones. A hip held earth for it touched the earth in falling. A hand touched a rib. Full of bullet holes like stars. The skulls were counted and earth laid down again over the stars.

"If you humbly say to someone, *forgive me,*
you'll burn the devils out."

And if I hold out my hands like water

Matei Voievod, nr. 33a, Sectorul 2, 021451 Bucharest. I'm terrified that I'll lose my notebook, so I'm publishing E.'s address here. Then if I lose it, I can buy her book and reconstitute everything.

In it, on page 41, I'll read: "Que l'homme ne soit pas toujours parlant, qu'il ait été et soit encore en-fant, voilà ce qui constitue l'expérience." Agamben, in translation. That there is a before-speaking, that we did not always speak, is this how experience is possible?

I have to return to the museum wall: the vertical field where sky and earth touch so deeply. On it, there is only a shirt.

The record of the body, an infinite outcry, an ethical subject

, a way of life.

And the child's rib in the birches of Oles'ko, a finger seeking ברוit

1 / 4

dearest trout: I would not be in this struggle if I did not
desire you.

Mea culpa, mea culpa, mea maxima culpa.

E.M., *2007*

There are persons who can speak no more, whose very names have vanished. Yet a name excised from the verge where it once lived still casts its sound on all who sleep there and enters their throats. "We are called *Grandyshyi*, for once there were *Grandyshyi* here..."

I remember the last sound my own mother called out in the city of my birth, in Calgary. A sigh, an interpellation that refused to articulate its word. I turned to her and spoke, as I was meant to.

Language *here*? Blind figuration? Грендишш? *Grandyshyi*?

There must be some other entry. It is not enough to have a body, so I would purge myself of it. But desire persists me. My mother sitting up in bed and me beside her. The intensity of her blind gaze. How can I talk about the face here? When a border leaves, *I* vanishes. *Máty*.

She carried a lantern out into the field to find her child. Its orange light stroked with hay.

A mother is the unmemntioable boundary
that can never come fully clear.

vanish
endure
[ripple]

Her brother years ago insisted she could not go back. "The village is gone; they burned it in the war." Who knew *who* burned it. A cousin once barred from Ukraine at the border said, "it didn't matter that I could not cross; there is no village."

But the village exists and the woman who walks alongside me on the soldiers' road, on the side of the river called Сторонка, points to where houses burned. The Polish houses were here, she said. And the church across the Davydivka, its grove since empty

She calls this grove not _____ but _____. (I don't catch the words)

We both know what occurred, *the glorious patriotic militia were called to fight the historic enemies of the people.*

(the museum in L'viv decrees it so)

What the villagers call that empty space of weeds, that grove or knoll
where my mother was baptized. Not _____, but _____.

Not церква but костъол, *kościół*, the word in the banished tongue

Shibboleth?   [can't hear you.]

Ear of corn?   [can't make out the word.]

She coughs. The body's own water pools in the crevice of her clavicle.
The wind ripples the lake so shallow now that no fish can winter
there.

(I are my own~~enemym~~emory)

[river]
[flick]
[flicker]

Unfortunately, censure has cut history up.

A wide experience by degrees sapped the faith reposed in my senses.

Silence at barbarity <mars> kills our souls in installments.

The wreck of culture, daughters observed brothers die in <to> great pang.

At first, language was cut off; closer, it pulled out eyes.

There, hope could not know we.

It is possible that all that coincides in the body are merely chimæræ.

In the passport <photo> the child <unstable signifier> defiant in the father's arms <thick hands> stares <outlive>.

"C'est sans doute là où la pensée se trouve."

Monster dozing in a person arises in extreme condition <poetry> and begins ravening. Faces remember people's names. Fear witness what they? Cough smoke from houses, this old church. Murdering <struggling> lasted repeated hours. That they survived <save> miracle.

Humiliation does not justify blood to trail out of skin. Horse reared up in my village. No one humiliated nobody in <to> my village. Different nations lived in agreement by centuries <ages>. But later part of my village completely crumbled, gone my other <polish> <local>.

Great fragment fallen to abyss and trees for tumulos cut down, pears, apples, forest birches. Therein lies the profound correspondence between the being and the thought.

Who they is. A Möbius problem. The woman in the village, too
young to have witnessed, saying: "Ukrainians sent by Stalin built
houses where the old had burned." And the official story, said
awkwardly. "Stalin sent the Poles to Poland."

Grove of trees:

Asile. Asyljm.
(we never touched or hurt the graves)
the empty grove
(we never touched or hurt the trees)

(i don't know why they did not come back to tend them)
костьол

~~Volove, Bibrka, forest, <Belżec)>~~

insert a map of culture here.   [   ]

Je suis moi-même une machine à écrire.

"…Ukrainian," said my mother.
"Polish," said my uncle, older.
"But Mom is Ukrainian," she insisted.
"Polish was what they taught in school!"
"Austrian," said my grandfather, gazing out at the soldiers' road.

"In secret on the mountain I tried to read the letters, for my parents
worried awake at night at what they told."
"One alphabet I could not read, they did not teach it in Canadian
school."

If only I could go backward, undo time. The trees out of narrow woods, and snows. Madre, matka, matyi, mama.

Yet to these shaking things that are my mysteries
my mother's answer still holds:
"we must press forward to the schools."

She sits up in bed and I embrace her. Later we are awake all night together one last time, me in the chair beside her, speaking ludicrously of banquets, of *pyrohy* filled with sour cabbage and mushrooms, waiting.

Across all is barren (ligature)
                    (wood)
                    (caldo)

cor de branco. remolacha. bors.

lumen.

This morning when I wake up from my dream of cabbage, I open my notebook and—my notes have vanished. It looks like my notebook, a black Moleskine bent down at the corner, with a page saved from *24 fun* in the back pocket: the Bucharest theatre schedule from August 1, its top scrunched.

But my notes are gone. Where once there were pages filled with my musings on the infinite, there is only this:

"There is a phantasmal poetry and a poetry of the seeing self. There is a miniaturized poetry and an aggrandizing poetry. And there is the poetry that doesn't want to be found. Stop desiring me! I have nothing to reveal. My withdrawal leaves no hole in the panorama." E.S. to E.M., Bucureşti, August 12.

This is crossed out, and there is, added in a hand not unlike E.S.'s:

Je vous avise de brûler la mémoire des cartes et de penser pour vous-même.

But what is a thinking being, *dearest trout*?

Res cogitans. Quid est hoc?

René Descartes, *1641*

I've decided to take E.M. for my experimental subject. She's here and she's a pest; she might as well serve some useful purpose. And she has an inner forum, and recalls an infancy, an *infans* before speaking.

As for me, I am better off without either.

E.M. in the trees and rain of Великі Глібовичі with the promise making her both light and heavy—*one of the last things I can do that my living mother wanted: to return her to the soil in Ukraine where she was born.* Testifying to the endurance of desire beyond any possibility of experience. The transfer of desire between bodies. Is this the beyond of experience? The beyond of borders?

Experience of "she"? A breach or symptom?

If experience requires entry into language, then we cannot experience death, for language ceases. There is no remnant.

Or there is. By taking her notebook, I make myself responsible. I myself become the restitution she is searching for. But I desert her. I left her a new notebook, and I'll fill hers on my own.

Halieutica

I am a thinking (conscious) thing, that is, a
being who doubts
I am certain that I am a thinking thing
in a manner or way of thinking
For when I think that a stone is a substance
although I conceive that I am a thinking and non-extended thing
merely in respect of our mode of thinking
since I am merely a thinking thing
since I am a thinking thing and possess in myself an idea of god
it is likewise a thinking being
in so far as I am a thinking being
I think it proper to remain here for some time in contemplation—

E.S.
București

The other disrupts the *I think*. Thus breaks with intentionality. Knowing any thing requires this breaking—a movement toward the exterior.

Is E.M. my exterior? I see her again, in the Museum café this time, fumbling a pen and glass. In her bag, that same spoon I saw her use to dig the earth at Great Hlibovychi, Великі Глібовичі. She buried something there, outside herself. Space and time, anachronic. Was it her way of making knowledge possible? To know any thing, time must go backward.

Look at her fumbling. What is her relation to experience now?

But of course she *is* experience, even as she is not fully captured by what she is thinking.

"Boreal forest and the north edge of aspen parkland."

Why did I write this just now?

(the scythes)

Epistulae

We get enough to eat here!

I remember paragraph, paragraph,
murmur.
The parents got up in the night.
I heard the sound of a rifle.
No, it was the stove.
The wood made a sound like an explosion,
jerked upright.
It was me sleeping.
Father outside in the dark with the gun, looking into the forest.
The quiet of deer.

Wealth to you! Wealth to you in the new
land!

E.S.
~~Великі Глібовичі~~
Huallen, Alberta

Aspen on the steep slope south and west with balsam poplar at small creek drainages. A few stands of mature white spruce on the hilltop plateau; along drainages on the north slope, birch rise over alder-willow shrubland mixed with foothills shrubs: mountain ash and thimbleberry.

Windbreak of green ash and laurel willow on the north of the field. Dozens of spruce at the south perimeter. It is a more moderate climate, apart from the impassable roads and wind.

Father and mother.
We had 23 crows and 3 ponies.

Due N. of Huallen, AB
(writing in the black Moleskine)
NW 14. 72. 9. W6

My intention was just to write at the desk in Bucureşti, but this notebook paper turns into a plant again damp with sap and fibre and breaks the nib. Perfumes anarchic tendency and a way with words, fallen down on crested birds.

"The smell of hay and the look of god"
the pen writes.

"We wept our gifts for you, dear mother, our treasures. Waking up in the night and wringing out the shirt. Even then, the tumour was growing in the blood."

(Tomasz's shadow bent long from the doorway to the forest, but it's just the noise of darkness and the gate banging shut in wind)

This notebook is arresting sleep (lying face-down in a pool of snow). When I look up, a siren, and the light of the ambulance flashes off the walls as it streaks down Matei Voievod in the dark…. but who does it carry? And repeatedly? E.M.? Has she eaten a peanut again?

Out the window I see not Matei Voievod, but the grande prairie of the South Peace west toward the raised shelf of the mountain never covered by the sheet of ice, they say. There the shut birches turn their buds to light the sky. I turn back to my room only when the clouds have rolled in and the mountain itself is obscured by May snow.

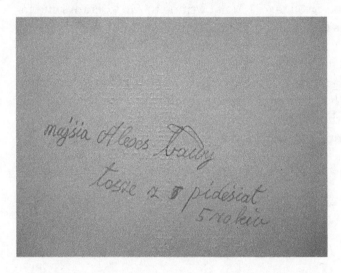

[Explore looking.]

The road carves north up the mountain then peters into a track past the farm. Ruts of mud deeper than a hand. Harsh light where the map is. "Louis" was how the English read the spires of "Tomas" handwritten in the ledger. Not one but eight ways to misspell his name. In '36, they tried to send his child from school because of back taxes (but they too owed taxes). "I am writing to Mr. Grentdys and in the event he does not conform you may have his children withdrawn from school."

Dans le halo de la mort, et là seulement, le *moi* fond son empire. That experience itself has its core in the impossibility of experience—a proximity to death—makes me realize that my project can but founder. Without an interior, this inner forum or sanctum, this beyond of being that founds being, there is no relation to death that can be "unresolved." Not only do I use E.M., but am forced to rely on her.

all this
might not be,
was relative, shaky

[register]
[trout]
[the most beautiful handmade desks ever seen]

It startles me when I find the second photo. It doubles the evidence. August, mere months after the emigration. White pinafore and clutching a mass card in front of Glowaski's (Novak's) log house, two quarter sections east along the Dane-ẕaa trail past the berry meadow, willow, arnica, balsam, sun. Her eyes are Asian, open.

"—One day, some piece of the book falls out like a stone that keeps the memory of a hallucinatory architecture to which it might have belonged. The stone still resonates and vibrates, it emits a kind of painful and indecipherable bliss, one no longer knows whose or for whom…
—Was the ~~postcard~~ photograph one of those stones?
—I don't know any longer." (D. *Points* 119, in spires of ink)

Boreal on the top of a mountain. Larkspur. Vagrant bears. The girl
rode the horse King to the log school called Mountain Trail built
where the road down the mountain crossed the migration route of the
Dane-ẕaa, later the Dawson Creek-Edmonton road. Other roads
impassable or rutted or just paths. The dance and Christmas pageant,
the singing news. Choral. In English, because of the fears. Outside,
children in gum boots on horses. Field day.

Winds (at home)

"relative"
"shaky"

[when i am gone, will you recall me, dearest trout?]

When the Indian doctor stood on the track at the forest edge, she said, waiting with a child (her interpreter) to be invited in, you knew you were really sick.

How did she know to come?
They lived there, they knew.

1. Balsam sap and bark boil down to tea or syrup, assuage the lungs. The inner bark succulent and sweet, ground as aspirin. The leaves soothe sores and bruises. 2. Mint leaves dried flat for headache. 3. Pine tar for cuts from brambles, disinfects but turns black (sent home from school for being dirty).

They sit in the chairs, mother and daughter, laughing—

Later, there is no cure with balsam or mint. No weapons, no shields, and almost no bodies. The shirt shimmers. She wipes water from her mother's clavicle. An ambulance light glows on their faces. The dice are rattling. The train stops in Hlibovychi. By starlight, the Dane-zaa woman sees them but cannot come.

Lying in the quiet room on the Rosedale bluff over the city, her mother counts trees. E.M.'s eyes see for two of them. E.M. turns the trees into numbers, and in the visual area of the brain, her *mama* sees. Lights of Calgary shimmer in the branches. *Arbres-aux-lueurs.* There are nine (9) trees, Mom

<siren>

"Beyond this door, time no longer exists."

In place of boreal forest, an object of experience:

> **Dexamethasone**
>   **4 mg**   **TAB**
> APO-DEXAMETHASONE
>
> Lot: HC5274
> Exp: 2007/10
> DIN: 02250055
> White pentagon
>
> **Calgary Health Region P**

The tumour in the brain presses: not to know. Numeration comes from 1 and 2, not 0 and 1. The 2 is silence, unanswerable without the 1.

How: a means. *Are*: exist. *You*: subject, other?

Yak shya mahsht, Mamai? Як ся маєте?

A cat purrs against the human leg, gets up, checks this very writing. Snow on a cold day.
Absence of 1. The infinite.

[My dearest trout...]

In the school at the foot of the mountain, they called me the Jew, her mother said at last, her eyes open, the wandering Jew.

Why, Mom; you weren't Jewish?

I don't know, she said.

When she woke again, she said: Maybe because I was always looking out the window. I wanted to learn everything. I wanted to leave the farm

(that history of sad letters)

When I married, the notice in Ottawa said I was from New York City
...

The healths!
The healths!

It occurs to me that I must write E.M.'s poems, since I can write none
of my own. Maybe once she's written them, or I have, she'll leave me
alone here. The expelled word _____
will be returned to its language, non-native but useable.

On the date before the date, time reverses. The village border
kindled now only
in the mouth, in the most intimate of conversations:

Jak się masz? E.M. asks M.I.M., bending close to her ear.
Я не знаю. <coalesce> Ya ne znayu, she whispers.

In one ear the anthropologist (daughter): how are you? meaning:
stay alive.
In the other the artist (mother): I don't know. meaning:
prepare to die, and transmit.

Ars Amatori

What for wind disperse
Not enough that it teach, it writer else.
I have reached a place <affirm> of sorrow
where I cannot know you, hope you.
Scratch marriage whole. Rich kinship <centuries> on those
verges, drying grain, they grew what bore fruit, sweet
earth emerge toward honour <shake>

The soldier road outside the door, shake their every field and light

I stand where light confess a field or gate:

Nation led to sticky sleep
Nation led to distance, forget
It must be on verges ukrainians sterroryzowani ≤ not

E.S.
NW 14.7

I've cast down the dice again. Wake up in the night drenched with
water. Oh, mine is an ongoing subseption more passive than any
passivity.

What would it be, Mother: wellspring or wound
if I too sank in the snowdrifts of Ukraine?

Was wär es, Mutter: Wachstum oder Wunde-
versänk ich mit im Schneewehn der Ukraine?

Paul Celan, *1943*

Consolatio ad L'vivium

E.M. with her expression lost continent evoke the course of history
today, E.M. captive of notions of philosophy and reconnaissant of
humanism her downfall equestre and same observing, E.M. the
notion of certainty in immediate experience via subjectivity
crumbling, E.M. expiate passages of history prejudicial or object
ceremony, one village mixed houses why mixed enemy foreign natural
obey E.M. diverge implore

(Instead of poems I will, like Ovid, write the letters here.)
Vel tibi composita cantetur Epistola voce: ignotum hoc aliis ille novavit opus.

(Will send her family the absent letters here, as ideology. No fact's
semblance to)

(the criminal revindications)

(the other adversary of Althusser)

:

E.S.
Bucureşti

*As for the letters, [J.D. The Post Card] I do not know if their reading is
bearable.*

Everyone comes from somewhere, Mom.
No, донечко, not everyone. Some people come from nowhere.

You came with a passport, мати, long before; you came from
somewhere.

When there was no one left, it became nowhere. There were no more
letters after the w

When they find the child up in the hill and bring her home.
Frightened of bears

The R&se Letters

by Grandmother Pound-Cake Rose

I woke up with blood in my mouth from reading.

handsewn book: 8 pages
condition: smirched
located: 2012 in a copy of The Unmemntioable
author: ~~Elisa Sampedrín~~
~~author: Grandmother Rose~~

EM moja droga,

The rest weep from we, who emerge in ways not Zmarł.
For <after> ten days of diseases Zmarł.
It asked, if <or> in wagon already <somebody> zmarł.
When it murder and it smoke <concealment> weary <tire>

It weep and extreme desperation has covered it outlawed from
the verge Ukrayina-Polska.
One people <people> weeped, others sang tender favourite homeland
farewell muzyka <voice>.
There were cries, screech <squeaks>, it weep.
The rest weep from we, who emerge.
There was one wall of weeping. And we have parted with <from> you

z.m.,
our verges grandmother <pound cake> Rose

Δopora EM,

In dark by fields resort to pathless tracks of where.
We pack at sunset, haste bedclothes on wagon throw mainly <dart>
and food.
We were shot from wood <stoned>, wounded <morning> become
stay.
Horse tested escape but brother shot and fell from horse.
Immediately we have moved to panic ways.

Though easter's past however spring was late we slept on snows.
And it has informed me, murderers will arrive this night and it must
run away.
Ukraine <poland>, even this people's, there was its own window for
they on world.
It has lost on verges of husband and son. And we have left our old
verges so.

our verges <borders> grandmother <pound
cake> Rose

beloved <love> EM,

They have woken us up, it awesome cries
from former opening once a face
Now sponge, it has not tongue

<Speech> about some they released <emit>
Imitate <manage> has tongue <speech> for <about>

They say something broken Polish
Here it scants something me.
Sound scants me near this city L'viv.

When Mom lived else, we bag for bread a bit сушений.
She said always, it will be need to save us from the hunger
can to be.

And it <her> gave bread it <him>
to <child>
and stopped of opening <famish> face of tears

з любов'ю
our verges grandmother <pound cake> Rose

It <I> love show be,

Porridge <morning> and ½ kg bread like clay for eating lived,
it left from person simply pasture <paste>.
Nine persons 1 slip bread, it was divide with tears to
desperation,
and something must put for mouths <self-service store>
We walk for sister from paring of potato, military paring few.
I have fallen ill on typhoid beyond fried cake in queue.
People <people> died from hunger daily.
It has meant from tree make cross her <its, she, it> mogiła <могила>
<tumulus> <mound>

Some <certain> strange internal joy has covered us which <who>
survivors else.

They released <refused> <emit>,

It left <obey, avow> our blessed verge

z.m.,
our verges grandmother <pound cake> Rose

<dear> EM,

To weep not lair <digest>,
but forbid me weep and noise.
There we do not go more, but forage food from foreign fields.
They saved us by cows before death hunger wettish <milk>.
People of <people of> whole areas of fields occupied and they
migrated so. They died on fields from hunger sit
ting mass. It dig great troughs and bury late <deceased> of
weep.

When there were food from foreign field ride assemble <collect,
convene> to lay camp <rest>.
It has lost lung, but it has survived more.
Where they are concealed and manner is unknown to me.

A verge runs deep and buried country was.
We who are lost <departed> love you to in each,

z.m.,
our verges grandmother <pound cake>
Rose

We have hidden with two girls unburning hidden sheet <metal>.

Roof has been fired <lit> and it burned fastly despite big snow.

There child further save being breathing.

One of they, they have hung on gate with nails young boy,

And they have deadened him, within his shirt.

When my mother has said my child suffocat ,.

experience is not what was undergone

but later, "me," saying it

<chair falld own>

it is write heavily me, to trace this

Fate has cared after explosion. It wrote further we have to L'viv with grandmother <pound cake>, for permit on departure for <from> Gestapo.

Question assign if <or> you are Niemką, are Pole? Grandmother <pound cake> has stated in village dialect my husband Pole. Officer has stated her <it>, it as you are married Pole, you can not leave it for <crowd> <robot> Reich. Reaction of grandmother <pound cake> not surprising then. As wall pale I have stood as I ear listen her. It has taken away voice and it cried you have killed husband, you have killed son. You want what else! Here we that not know what else meet <face>. German officer after this word attack to unexpected completely her. Suddenly <snap> Niemiec in April.

Crippled soundly by Niemiec, Rose <she> have voice but faultless she left to heaven <providence> too soon. There have <be> no tomb of grandmother <pound cake> in <to> Rose.

Pink tomb of son of Mozart, yes! Czechs in old cemetery, still! And on all sides, refugee mounds and tumulæ of soldiers. Then <sweat> it has answered bitter ground:

There verges our are finished for I. There verges our are finished for I exactly.

It <she> has not survived grandmother <pound cake> your war.

droga Anastazjo,

I know one more method to cross the border. Take a bottle of horilka and drink it with the sellers of birds.

The way they do it then is that they take you to Przemyśl, but only on market day, they give you cages with birds and they tell you to go with them as if you were their helpers; and they will teach you what to do.

At the verge the officers distract in song of birds.

Then fly as you will in the wagons to Antwerp. Look up for stars. Where light meets earth, the land rolls back to ache of verges but do not with it turn.

They say in Antwerp the fastest steamship goes.

Experience appears in this world as a birth. A birth which takes as assistants sky and earth and the water and wood and mountains and the clouds. Experience does not come out of the mind or imagination but from a deep and irrecusable need. It rents the entire person.

On the stove tiles: Napoleon, birch leaves, deer leaping, magnolias, birds, horns, mermaids. We are the heirs of these traces, oh my brothers. In us they are the sign of the whole.

[dearest trout]

the unmemntioable

I swam for us both. I did not swim. *Dear
trout*. The shimmertree swam.

Ich schwamm für uns beide. Ich schwamm nicht.
Der Flimmerbaum schwamm.

Paul Celan, *1963*

the unmemntioable

L'arbre aveugle vers l'arbre étend ses membres sombres,
Et cherche affreusement l'arbre qui disparaît...

Paul Valéry

1

when i stood and wept before the icons
of the brain
the calf was sleeping

*

i found the most wonderful street of lindens
i wandered in parks and gardens
in disturbances of green
in nettles
in the most untended gardens in Europe
my surprise was that i write in english

2

where the calf had lain down in its skin to sleep
it was a horse then
leaping sideways
shaking the shadow of soil

no leaf bract moving

*

fell slowly from the saddle
its smell of wet leather
in treed disturbances of green

3

what names did i give
those lonely words
before they repeated me?

aside from an outcry
a task of home
my interior vigilant naturally as a horse
on scented pavement

schmerz

*

my throat awake in the street of lindens
we both have known a grace of horses
our plea

to cross the soil

4

i woke up from that sleep then
honoured her

and only wept now, eight months later

*

when i stood before the horse
whose speech foreshortened
is all throat
faceless in the linden city
its right ear sewn inward

5

the unmemntioable
hills horses dreams trout yews _____

unmentionable

*

linden stamens yellowed fallen
rest silent on wet roofs
where we have reigned

6

as love is, home is
(the name of Heidegger appears nowhere)
at the icons of the brain, i stood and wept

in veneration

and shouldered her as horse
as welter
being

*

one last time please lift us skyward
calf and stamen

7

suddenly we are bound by laws that avow the body

habeas corpus ad subjiciendum,
"tu devras avoir un corps à montrer"

je te voue mon corps

*

an enigma in the cells
plasma cells yews horses

a walk in light on a street of lindens

the inside
of the brain
lit blue

its icon that they turned in 3D blue on-screen to show me

i wanted to be brave then / to open us / to waking fully

8

in the book its throat cut wide by a maddened robber
the boy held tight the horse's neck
and pressed a hand there
to beg its body not to die

there was a river
and clay to staunch the flow

we have neither

how many times i have written this river before you
(throat i touch with just a gaze)
(aches me)
(i raise up these arms)
(extend my hand)

oh

mom, you are this horse
we are this calf
i am this girl this boy

*

FORBIDDEN LINES

"in the past week i thought hopefully about the future"
"it's beautiful this oh doubling, this freeing and dislodging of time"
"then you can pick rhubarb from this very garden"
"in the sky to us now where footpath is field"
"our mad telluric limbs"
"the printed band worn to represent the true length and girth and the
measure of her foot"
"where the calf has shuddered, sleeping"
i found the most astonishing street of lindens
i wandered in parks and gardens
in disturbances of green
in rain on roses
in camadas of stamens blown from trees
in the lush arboreal majesty of june
in the paseo along the rivers and in the camposantos
in the most untended gardens in Europe
i wake with my arms and opened shoulder
the grass grows high and viburnum blooms and linden stamens fall as rain

Berlin, Europe
June 2007

,,

i sew the alphabet shut too
a to b, facing
ab to cd, facing
o to a, facing
i to u, o, un
faced

e
the unmemntioable

~~dignity, observation, doubt~~
face us:
je t'avoue mon corps

,,

[Найдорожча фореле] перед тобою я і моє тіло.

jocurile de noroc

In the innermost core of blinded love,
which is not and must never, *dear t,* be realized,
lives the demand to be unblinded.

Er erkennt, daß im Innersten der verblendeten Liebe,
die nichts davon weiß und nichts wissen darf,
die Forderung des Unverblendeten lebt.

Theodor Adorno, *1951*

I'm awake, rubbing my eyes. Poring over the map of Great Hlibovychi, I look for signs: they had slipped between the boards at night and run into the Ernsdorf Forest. What were they thinking? Even the forest Jews who used to come at night for food had not come. The birches were silent. There was just the distant sound that air makes when there is no sound. An undifferentiated grey sky that morning. The road a strip of light not invented yet. Marja. Alex. Herm.

* * *

In the dream, I was not able to answer the question: are you right- or left-handed? So I said both, but that I could not write with my left hand.

Animals asleep. A thinking man with a flying fish and a thinking man above, and representations of togas.

(so much of history is language here
(even the telling tells of language
(my right hand aching
(syllables seen with my own eyes in a plaster frieze of war

* * *

In 1944, Soviets seized an UPA North order dated February 11, which said: Freedom for the Peoples! Freedom for the Individual! Liquidate Polish traces:
a) Destroy all walls of churches and other Polish sites of worship.
b) Destroy trees growing near homes so that no trace remains that anyone had lived there (do not destroy fruit trees by roads).

c) Before Nov 25, 1944, destroy all houses formerly inhabited by Poles (if Ukrainians are living in them, it is imperative that the houses should be taken apart anyway and turned into dugouts; if not, the homes will be burned and people who live in them will have nowhere to spend the winter). We alert you once more that if anything remains that is Polish, Poles will have claims to our lands.

* * *

What can I make of these side roads of grief? Ache is our alphabet, it has jewels and jewels. Don't ever let them tell you "decorum"! Or forget. I walk on Strada Plantelor in Bucharest, exiled, lonely in three languages. Strangely humid, for it rained hard earlier. The fires and dogs, leaves and dogs. Lilacs. Old women like my mother, and what a 19th century here! The fires. But there are no fires. Mobile phones and cigarettes. The new breed of dog, made out of all dogs. "I'm not then innocent."

* * *

16 August. Sunt bolnavă, a kind of congestion in the head. Need ColdFX and much more water. I struggle as best I can to Strada Matei Voievod where E.S. lives but her address is empty. Street dust on the window and lumber stacked on the floor inside, as if for renovations. Along the back wall, shelves of greying hats, one space vacant. Left-handed in Bucharest—for how long?

Here where each small territory of beauty is staked out, perfected, then hidden, is there use for metaphor? À *peine nous admettons le réel.*

* * *

I wake still drunk on dreams at noon. Water. ColdFX. *DaDa* is still going strong a few streets away, one point on a four-point nexus: Amsterdam, Αθήνα, Bucureşti, 東京. I sat at one of the red barstools, spoke—cafea, vă rog—and was served by a young man in white as if my accent didn't matter and "cafea, vă rog" was how one ordered coffee anywhere. As if Bucharest had stopped being in Turkey, as if we'd shaved off our shtetl beards, even the women, as if small colours and joy existed, and no need to flee from Gara de Nord to Zurich.

So E.S. has vamoosed. In her neighbourhood, the dogs, lumina de dimineaţă, the church and women cleaners with brooms in the park sweeping cigarette ends, and later Roma men and the dice game and more cigarette ends. And this cold. *Timpul învaţa pe cei făra şcoală.*

* * *

Bucharest, I said to Răzvan, the film critic, when we met for coffee, is a microcosm of the world. As B. changes, so will the world, for better or for worse. So I come here; I walk on Str. Negustori, Merchant Street, on Plantelor, the Street of Plants, on Matei Voievod, Prince Matthew Street. I wait, and draw my own conclusions:

"A lot of aching beauty."

* * *

On Merchant Street, instead of lost pet posters, I read posters for lost old people. Or for people with tumours, needing intercession.

Above the cluttered bar where I write these words, a framed photo of azure water at a resort on the Black Sea, the Romanian Riviera. The waitress is standing in the doorway, a figure outlined in white light. "A lot of aching beauty." My translation of Bucharest: "The dark star brightens." *Luceafărul se soreşte*.

"My offence was that I had eyes," wrote Ovid long ago, from Tomis on the Black Sea. Sometimes we are blinded by what we cannot see.

* * *

Finally I brave my fears and go back to the Museum for there I can explore looking. In the room that protects the wooden church, I seek out the shirt. It's spread on the wall now in an elaborate cross with the neck rounded stiffly. On an empty stand where an explanatory plaque would fit nicely, there is a typed note: "Nici noi nu mai ştim ce era scris aici. Ceva frumos despre timp..." *Even we no longer know what was written here. Something beautiful about time....*

If E.S. is gone, is her research on experience ended? Yet if you dream of Elisa by that wooden church, it means she is close by, says Chus Pato.

* * *

I can't believe it. I saw her. In the warren of rooms in Palatul Parlamentului, third floor. I have to tell Chus. An exhibition of women video artists. She's in a blue anorak and beige jeans, and sings the song my mother made me sing as a child to make myself stop crying. Over and over, just as my mother insisted. Around her on park benches, people wake up, panic at her warble and microphone, leave.

Keep on the sunny side
Always on the sunny side
Keep   ”   ”   ”   ”   of life
It will help us every day
It will brighten all the way
If we keep on t.s.s.o.l.

Julia Weidner, „Keep On" „Mergi mai departe", 2003, 8'33

* * *

It startles me to see her on video. That's *my* grandmother she's describing. And it was *my* mother in the cancer hat. She can't subsume what doesn't belong to her.

* * *

What is inside, what is outside. What bears worth. What is a noise in the mouth. There are people just north of Bucharest never conquered who still laugh at death in strict ceremonies of pandemonium and refutation. I wait in Caru'cu Bere on Stavropoleos Street for tripe soup with a long hot pepper on the side. R. arrives with an envelope for me, sent to his office at Time Out București.

When I pull out the first item, I recognize the turned-down black cover. I turn to the last page and read in a curious hand: "Fleeting glimpse of E.M. on Str. Negustari. Wearing my socks." I glance toward the floor, startled: I had taken them out of my suitcase on Merchant Street that morning.

My notebook.

* * *

Dear Chus: In Bucharest there is a street—Matei Voievod—where, when you cross it, time stops on one side and starts on the other.

* * *

Dear Chus: everything I had dreamed turned out to be made of paper. The skin was an organ that suffered in silence the rays, the scourges, the cuts of trees and medicine. In Hlibovychi in 1922, the war was over but the repressions escalated. Predeceased by her father Oleks, now with more children, my grandmother Anastasia emigrated with Tomasz in 1929, to NW14.72.9.W6. Riding down the south side of the mountain, the side with a road, the smallest daughter, my mother, went to school.

Forderung. "We must press forward to the schools."

In the innermost core of blinded love, which is and must never be realized, a woman is trying to open her eyes to see.

* * *

Though my mother is gone, her face still claims me. In the morning I write wearing her cancer hat. I wear her Western belt to Whitehorse. In my pocket, she stands at the summit cairn in Wonder Pass with her friends the nurses. They wear anoraks and sunhats. Maybe one day, as she did, I will wear her blue ribbed hat, the knitted one, as hair.

* * *

Dear Chus: Elisa is doing theatre again, on the grassy knoll of Bucharest behind Palatul Parlamentului, in the burned-out building on Str. Plantelor, at the shawarma stand on Bul. Brătianu. She brings a pad of paper and draws daisies till the pad is full of petals. It is so 1970. But she has a fever. It turns out (maybe) she's been ill. She has these crazy sweats. Unbearable. They come day and night. They leave pools of water in the teaspoon space of the clavicle. It makes me think of sleeping behind my grandmother's stove, this being so hot.

Then "keep on the sunny side."
There is no more time to research experience.
The light flashes off the wall and the passing siren cuts the glass.

* * *

My notebook is full of Elisa's strange tabulations:

"Cel mai frumos lucru din lume este soarele." (1970)

"The sky is god's astronaut." (1907)

"Much of the sun and moon's journey is difficult for they must pass through stone; I see but the part where they cross the window." (1944)

"There are more than seven stars." (1907)

"When you look to the first star of evening and wish, it will come true." (1944)

"God placed the Milky Way so the conqueror Traian could get back to Rome." (1944)

"Language is no bone to be left to bleach in the wind." (2009)

* * *

I dreamed Elisa has abandoned theatre in order to reinvent things that need reinventing. Last night it was "money"; in the dream it looked like squares of paisley cloth.

I told Chus, who wrote back: I've always loved Hindu cloth, cloth with the name of a street, paramecial cloth; to wrap ourselves in such cloth is to become imperceptible; Capital passes through us and thus we make it vanish. Goodnight to you, and to Elisa who somewhere sleeps.

Tonight in my dream, E.S. invented the bottle opener. It wasn't any different from any other bottle opener. Why did she see the need to create it? It is as if theatre must now be small enough to fit in your hand, and the body is its proscenium. I look down at my socks again.

Now I know what she is doing.

* * *

We talk on Facebook as Chus doesn't get my email any more: her server blocks all messages from me in Romania. I'm writing spam, it seems.

Tonight, Elisa invents "red shoes". They are joined at the heel, making it impossible to walk anywhere without tipping over. My funny valentine, I thought, waking. My dearest trout.

* * *

I like to wake up in my city at 5:30 and sit at the café table by the window. I am awake when no one else is, drinking coffee, feeling the variousness of the body's demises but quietly glad. Beside me is the cancer hat. For a long time after she died, it carried the soft perfume of her head—the smell of a baby. As if my mother's thoughts were still in it —not brain-tumour thoughts but the thoughts that worked despite the brain tumour, trying to straighten out the world that the tumour ruined. How many trees are out there? she'd ask me. My ever-mathematical mother. Numbers order the outside world but were also a kind of intimacy with it.

* * *

There are nine (9) trees. *Arbres-aux-lueurs*. The body itself is exile. Numbers construct a world where trees can shimmer, and will. The forest

* * *

Rain in the street below. Morning after an earthquake. I wake suddenly with an image of trout and red pepper. Too much fever to leave the bed, though I'd felt it quaking. Dead still now. No air, no ColdFX, and a head with a carpet in it. A bit better than yesterday but, oh, tomorrow, somehow, I need the energy to get to Constanţa, to the ruins of Tomis. I have a message for Ovid, from Jeny Tripas.

* * *

Jeny Tripas: don't lose heart, Erín, I assure you Elisa is at the poker tables in the casino at Constantza. Take care of that cold.

* * *

Finally the cough is receding. Thinking in Constanţa of what Chus (Jeny) says of Ovid—that he was an erotic poet and couldn't thus live without a city and a court. Being confined is the worst punishment for an erotic poet. Or was C. talking of E.S.?

Whom I saw again. On the seaside promenade near the city's magnificent *Cazinou*. On the eastern finis terrae of the Latin world, Tomis at the brink of Pontus Euxinus, Fortunate Sea. The Romans left ruins here. Now a breakwater of cast concrete leads far into the black waters, which are blue. I walk out on the long dock toward the casino. It looks like a wedding cake. E.S. doffs her fez. We stand a moment, both gazing at the Black Sea, the most ancient landscape in Europe, altered daily by the youngest, the delta of the Danube. Ovid's antique anguish is palpable here, his relegation for writing *Ars Amatori* and for witnessing what he cannot speak of. "I am here because of my eyes," he wrote. But unlike Ovid, Elisa is not one for *Tristele*. She knows what she sees.

* * *

My mother arrived at this sea too, blind, the year before her illness. Her attraction to casinos was well known, due to their intense numeration.

Then from Constanţa on a ship to Odesa with my cousin (who had once looked over the border), she touched the soil of Ukraine for the first and only time since her emigration as a child before the war.

* * *

What will Elisa do—swim? Be devoured by birds? Sit on a park bench here too with a microphone and in a stupid anorak singing "Keep on the sunny side"?

* * *

She had sent a postcard via Time Out as well. It was when she realized on Matei Voievod, amid the hats and lumber, that experience = not just the proximity of death, but love. Love not solely in the presence of the beloved, but in the presence of the world—the world, what is the world—from one side of the old imperium, the western shore of Gallæcia and the Styx where Chus Pato was born, to the other, Pontus, the inner sea, where Ovid lived in exile. North of here, I crossed my mother's path on the verges of the eastern Galicia, Halychyna, Western Ukraine. The path of a child (that unstable signifier). Though my mother has gone to rest at Great Hlibovychi and above Wonder Pass at Mt. Assiniboine, paths can still be crossed. There is still a lot of aching beauty. Yet songs can still be sung.

* * *

When I reach the end of the pier, E.S. is already there. I recognize her socks, and the fez pushed flat on top like the cancer hat. The casino looms as ship, chasm, meringue behind her.

At the verge of the Black Sea, it's suddenly clear: for the casino, Elisa had invented money, the bottle opener and red shoes. So she could rattle the dice and cast them down unread. Now I follow her gaze into the distance to the right at the line of loading cranes on the horizon—like huge awkward trees—at the harbour of Agigea where Canalul Morții brings Danube waters sideways to the sea. A human feat of death and engineering.

I turn around, my back up against the huge locked door. The casino is shut, abandoned. Where Elisa had been standing, broad steps spread out infinitely white, pointing back to the city. On them, no one. Just a stray dog that fell asleep in the shade, now getting a headache in the blinding sun. The dog formed of all dogs, its eyes shut. Sirius, dog star. Here, too, the earth touches deeply the sky.

* * *

There are other ways to win your wager, Chus wrote. I think she knew all along the casino was closed.

* * *

Its building is majestic, otherworldly, at the end of the pier. A vast icing holding emptiness. A body turned inside out to display its organs of beauty. A constellation risen from the earth. There are clouds above it. Here touch and sight merge. Presence excludes, ultimately, all infinity and all transcendence.

Elisa's postcard had said simply: "All bets are off, Erín." In the envelope with my notebook she'd also placed her Edmund Burke (1943) *On the Beautiful and the Sublime* and Ovid, not *Ars amatori* but *Tristele* in Romanian (1957), bearing a library stamp from Suceava near the border with Ukraine. This and a tiny purse from Guatemala in which there's a bit of soil and crushed grass. I recognize it: my mother's purse. I know I must go north to the grande prairie, to Anastasia's tomb in the cemetery down the mountain and across the plain from NW14.72.9.W6, to restore the earth to her. I'll mail Ovid's *Tristele* back to the library in Suceava, from Bucharest, before I leave.

And when I close this book, which I will do for experience lies outside it, a gate will open. Time, *timp*, stopped on one side, will start on the other. Buds will explode into birch leaves and bend the light of the sun. The hills of Hlibovychi and Huellen will rise in restless stems of grain and flowers. There are just two things different from when I set out: *All bets are off*, and I can write again with my own right hand.

Îndrăznește, dearest trout! Take courage!

[Explore looking.]

Upward and directly in front, where both eyes operate, there is depth perception. Toward the rear and sides, vision is monocular: no depth. The cone of the world widens as it extends upward from the iris; on the surface the diameter of its opening is twice the depth of swimming. The only blind spots are directly behind and under. The eyes see colour as well as do human eyes, though more vividly in the yellow to blue wavelengths, which travel better in water.

Human ears in air use fluid for balance. Theirs, in fluid, use calcified stone. The three-chambered internal ear picks up sound so well that when a woman stops writing and sets down her pen, the sound is easily audible to any trout across the lake.

Sensory input received by a Rainbow is estimated to be 500-800 times more acute than that received by a human.

[dearest trout]

116

Written between June 2007-May 2011 in Montréal, L'viv, Vilnius, Calgary, Grande Prairie, Bucharest, Constanţa, Berlin and Rio de Janeiro, and indebted to:
Patrick Desbois, *Holocaust by Bullets:* http://www.holocaustbybullets.com
Orest Subtelny, *Ukraine, A History.*
Shimon Redlich, *Together and Apart in Brzeżany: Poles, Jews, Ukrainians, 1919-1945.*
Kate Brown, *A Biography of No Place.*
Mila Sternberg-Mesner, *Light From The Shadows.*

Ovid, *Tristia.* tr. P. Green. Chus Pato, *Hordas de Escritura.* Paul Celan, *Der Niemandsrose,* tr. M. Broda as *La rose de personne.* Cormac McCarthy, *The Crossing.* Jacques Derrida. Emmanuel Lévinas. C.D. Wright. Denis Diderot. Christian Boltanski. Judith Butler. Giorgio Agamben. Jean-Luc Nancy. René Descartes. Georges Bataille.

Muzeul Ţăranului Român, Bucureşti. South Peace Archives, Grande Prairie AB and archivist Mary Nutting. Julia Weidner: http://www.youtube.com/watch?v=irZfl0AbjrE; "The Extraordinary Rainbow Trout," R. Newman:
http://www.bcadventure.com/ronnewman/rainbow.phtml
Not used for I read it later, but quick nonpolemic background by Timothy Snyder:
http://www.nybooks.com/blogs/nyrblog/2010/feb/24/a-fascist-hero-in-democratic-kiev/
For information on the Dane-zaa ("the real people") or Beaver people and to learn about the songs of their dreamers:
http://www.virtualmuseum.ca/Exhibitions/Danewajich/english/index.html

Warmest thanks to: Oana Avasilichioaei for incisive editing and correcting at critical stages, and to Jars Balan, Anthony Burnham, Oksana Dudko, Georges Gamache, Emeren García, Lazer Lederhendler, Belén Martín Lucas, Bill Moure Jr., Chus Pato, Florin Dan Prodin, Elisa Sampedrín, Vida Simon, Adam Sol, Răzvan Ţupa.
Thanks to Lana Turner, Eleven Eleven, The Nation, LIT Magazine (USA); Critical Quarterly (UK); Beautiful Outlaw Press, no press, The Capilano Review, cv2, Rhubarb and Centre A Gallery (Canada). Merci to *Conseil des arts et des lettres du Québec*, Canada Council, SLS (Summer Literary Seminars) and uOttawa for travel monies, a grant, a brief teaching gig and a one-term residency that allowed this work to be created.

Dear brothers: everything.
Dearest trout:_____.

In memory of Isak Messer, photographer of Bibrka, near Great Hlibovychi, Ukraine who surely took the one photo I had of my mother as a child, with her parents and siblings, for their passport to Canada. I see my child mother through Messer's eyes. He and his family perished in the Shoah: in the Bibrka ghetto, in Bełżec on August 13, 1942, at the extermination near Volove on April 13, 1943, at the brickworks a day or so later, or in the forest. Also in memory of Anastasia Hamulyak and Tomasz Grędysz, who left their native Ukraine in 1929 to farm in northern Alberta where there were no wars. Finally, in honour of my mother м.і.м., Марія Грендиш, to whose 'inner forum' I owe this book.

Experience appears in this world as a birth. A birth which takes as assistants sky and earth and the water and wood and mountains and the clouds. Experience does not come out of the mind or imagination but from a deep and irrecusable need. It rents the entire person.

About the Author

Erín Moure is a Canadian poet who writes in English, multilingually. In her recent *O Resplandor* and—in collaboration with Oana Avasilichioaei—*Expeditions of a Chimæra*, poetry is hybrid, and emerges from or in translation and collaboration. Moure also translates poetry into English, from several romance languages, and has signed translations of Quebec poets Nicole Brossard (with Robert Majzels) and Louise Dupré from French, Galician poets Chus Pato and Rosalía de Castro from Galician, Chilean Andrés Ajens from Spanish, and Fernando Pessoa from Portuguese. Her essays on reading and writing, *My Beloved Wager*, appeared in 2009. She performs and speaks nationally and internationally on poetry and translation, and her work has been honoured with awards almost as often as it has been received with puzzlement. *The Unmemntioable*, her 16th book of poetry, is an investigation into subjectivity and experience in western Ukraine and the South Peace region of Alberta. Moure lives primarily in Montreal.

From reviews of Moure's previous book, *O Resplandor*:

"Moure has composed a joyfully aching, tough, and vulnerable poetry of lyrical splendour, a liberated culmination of the transgressive, language-based poetics that has so richly, powerfully, and playfully hinged her poetry, essays and translations to date." — *Winnipeg Free Press*

". . . a layered, erudite, tender book, aspiring, inspiring, declarative, a book of principled assertion and lovely description." — *Influency Salon*

"*O Resplandor* is an elegy to love, a testament to friendship . . ." — *Matrix Magazine*

"A new book by Erín Moure is always an exciting event in Canadian literary history . . . this is a tour-de-force of lyric writing." — *Prairie Fire*

"*O Resplandor* is gloriously indefinable. Deeply layered with voices, translations, and lyric, the text crimps, collages, blurs and smudges. Indeed, *O Resplandor* delightfully confounds the reader's expectations on many levels. The text is in turns playful, philosophical, serene, restrained, and rambunctious. The pacing of the book is virtuosic." — Quebec Writers' Federation

"*O Resplandor* is nothing less than an attempt at epistemology . . . It makes for a remarkable reading experience: the utterance of a ghost, voiced by the phantasmagoria of language itself." — *Harvard Review*

"Heady, heartbreaking, visionary — the words to describe *O Resplandor* come one after the other, from their spiritual home in the mouth." — *Event Magazine*

« L'expérience ne peut être communiquée si des liens de silence, d'effacement, de distance, ne changent pas ceux qu'elle met en jeu. » Georges Bataille, *1954*

Льольові Нотатки

Field Notes

Лольові Нотатки

Field Notes